GETTING TO KNOW
THE U.S. PRESIDENTS

J A M E S
BUCHANAN

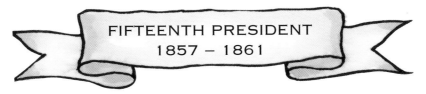

FIFTEENTH PRESIDENT
1857 – 1861

WRITTEN AND ILLUSTRATED BY MIKE VENEZIA

CHILDREN'S PRESS®
A DIVISION OF SCHOLASTIC INC.
NEW YORK   TORONTO   LONDON   AUCKLAND   SYDNEY
MEXICO CITY   NEW DELHI   HONG KONG
DANBURY, CONNECTICUT

Reading Consultant: Nanci R. Vargus, Ed.D., Assistant Professor, School of Education, University of Indianapolis

Historical Consultant: Marc J. Selverstone, Ph.D., Assistant Professor, Miller Center of Public Affairs, University of Virginia

Photographs © 2005: Art Resource, NY: 28 (John Henry Brown/Smithsonian American Art Museum, Washington, DC, U.S.A.), 26 (National Portrait Gallery, Smithsonian Institution, Washington, DC, U.S.A.); Corbis Images: 18, 21, 22, 24, 32 (Mathew B. Brady Studio), 3 (Charles Fenderich/Bettmann); Gilcrease Museum, Tulsa, Oklahoma: 30 (The Coming and Going of the Pony Express, by Frederic Remington); Lancaster County Historical Society, Lancaster Pennsylvania: 10; Mercersburg Academy: 6; Missouri Historical Society, St. Louis, MO: 23 (Dred Scott, by Louis Schultze); North Wind Picture Archives: 8 (Nancy Carter), 25; Stock Montage, Inc.: 27.

Colorist for illustrations: Dave Ludwig

Library of Congress Cataloging-in-Publication Data

Venezia, Mike.
  James Buchanan / written and illustrated by Mike Venezia.
      p. cm. -— (Getting to know the U.S. presidents)
   ISBN 0-516-22620-7 (lib. bdg.) 0-516-25486-3 (pbk.)
1. Buchanan, James, 1791-1868-—Juvenile literature. 2. Presidents—-United States—
Biography-—Juvenile literature. I. Title.
  E437.V46 2005
  973.6'8'092–dc22

                          2004022574

1 2 3 4 5 6 7 8 9 10 R 14 13 12 11 10 09 08 07 06 05

A portrait of President James Buchanan

James Buchanan was the fifteenth president of the United States. He was born in Cove Gap, Pennsylvania, on April 23, 1791. When James became president in 1857, the United States needed a strong leader. People hoped President Buchanan would be the one who could keep the nation together and prevent a civil war.

In 1857, the people of the United States were splitting into two groups. On one side were people from the northern states, who were against slavery. On the other side were people from the southern states. Many southerners used black slaves to run their farms and plantations.

Americans felt very strongly about slavery, and both sides were becoming angrier and angrier. President Buchanan knew how bad things were and feared that a war might start because of it. Unfortunately, he took very little action to fix the problem, and pretty much let everyone down.

James Buchanan was born in a log cabin in Cove Gap. Before long, his family moved into a large, two-story brick house. James' father became very successful running a trading post that sold goods to settlers who were heading west.

James Buchanan was born in this log cabin.

James' father made the first floor of the family home into a store. James went to work in the store as soon as he could see over the counter. Mr. Buchanan cared a lot about details and taught his son to be the same way. James learned to keep track of every piece of merchandise and every cent that came into the store.

Buchanan went to Dickinson College in Carlisle, Pennsylvania.

James' mother taught her son to read at an early age. He became an excellent student in grammar school and college. James got into a lot of trouble at Dickinson College, though. His classmates were more interested in goofing off than in studying. James wanted to be part of the group, so he decided to be a troublemaker, too.

Even though James Buchanan kept his grades up, he was almost expelled from college for his bad behavior. In order to graduate, James had to promise to stay completely out of trouble. In 1809, James was happy to finish up and leave Dickinson College. His teachers and professors were even happier.

Now James was ready to choose a career. His mother was very religious. She wanted him to become a church minister. James' father, however, thought his son would make a better living as a lawyer. James decided to go along with his father's wishes. He traveled to Lancaster, Pennsylvania, to study with and assist a well-known lawyer there.

As a young man, James studied and practiced law in Lancaster, Pennsylvania.

Lancaster was an exciting city. At the time, it was the capital of Pennsylvania. James was tempted to go out at night and party, but his father kept writing letters reminding James to work hard. Mr. Buchanan didn't want a replay of his son's college days.

James listened to his father and worked harder than ever. For fun, James would often walk through the forest, reciting laws out loud and making up imaginary court cases. His only audience was the forest animals. After three years, James passed his law exam and opened a law office of his own.

James didn't get much business at first, though. A friend suggested that it might be a good time for him to try to get elected to a government job. James liked the idea. He decided to run for Pennsylvania state representative. James entered the election and won! Mr. Buchanan worried that James was making a mistake by getting into politics.

James Buchanan knew that politics was right for him. He was always good at fighting for ideas. He had always loved joining in on the political discussions that took place in his father's store.

He had been a good debater in college, too. James met lots of important people as a state representative. Many of them became clients and contacts when James returned to his law business.

James became known for winning his cases by spending hours arguing over the smallest details to convince people he was right. Soon James became quite wealthy.

James Buchanan was the only president who never married. As a young man, he did fall in love once with a beautiful girl named Ann Coleman. They even became engaged. Because of some misunderstanding, Ann decided to break off the engagement. Soon after this happened, Ann died unexpectedly.

James was so upset that he never fell in love again. Instead, he put all of his time and effort into politics and public service. James did extremely well. He was very popular and was known for his honesty and knowledge of the U.S. Constitution. James spent almost forty years doing various government jobs before becoming president.

SOUTHERN CHIVALRY — ARGUMENT versus **CLUB'S.**

In 1856, pro-slavery Congressman Preston Brooks attacked and badly injured anti-slavery Senator Charles Sumner.

After serving in the Pennsylvania House of Representatives, James Buchanan went on to become a U.S. Congressman, and then a minister to Russia. In 1834, he became a U.S. senator. He was secretary of state under President James Polk, and later was appointed ambassador to Great Britain. While James was away in Great Britain, the argument over slavery became more and more explosive.

Some Congressmen were so angry with each other that they even got into fights during meetings! Members of James' political party, the Democratic Party, were fighting among themselves, too. They couldn't agree on whom they should choose to run for president in the next election. When James returned home, he seemed like a good choice. James had lots of experience, and no one was angry with him—yet.

In 1856, James Buchanan ran for president of the United States. He won against the Republican Party's candidate, John Frémont. Now it was up to President Buchanan to figure out how to keep the country from splitting apart.

It wasn't going to be easy. A few years before James became president, it had been decided that settlers in the territory of Kansas could make up their own minds if they wanted to allow slavery or not.

An illustration showing a gunfight in "Bleeding Kansas" between abolitionists and supporters of slavery

What had seemed like a fair solution turned into a real mess. Southerners who wanted slavery and northerners who hated it poured into Kansas to try to convince people which way to vote. Soon serious fighting broke out, and the area became known as "Bleeding Kansas."

An illustration showing James Buchanan's presidential inauguration in 1857

Just two days after James Buchanan became president, an important court case was decided. It was called the Dred Scott Decision. Dred Scott was a black slave who decided to sue his owner for freedom. This case made it all the way to the highest court of all, the U.S. Supreme Court. Many people were surprised when the court said Dred Scott had no right to sue anyone.

As a slave, Dred Scott wasn't considered a citizen of the United States. In fact, he was considered only a piece of property. As unbelievable as it seems today, the Supreme Court at that time pretty much said that slaves were the same as a kitchen table, coffee pot, or horse and wagon.

A portrait of Dred Scott by Louis Schultze

Slaves being auctioned at a slave market in the South in the 1850s

As far as President Buchanan was concerned, the Supreme Court had the final say. If a slave was property, and the U.S. Constitution gave people the right to own property, then that should be the end to any more arguments on the subject.

James Buchanan wasn't for slavery. In fact, he said he hated the idea of it. However, in order to keep the United States from splitting in two, he encouraged everyone to go along with the court's decision and start getting along better. Instead of getting along, people in the North were outraged! They thought the Supreme Court was wrong and threatened to ignore its decision.

An abolitionist speaking out against slavery in Boston in the 1850s

A portrait of
John Brown

    Things kept getting worse and worse
between the North and South. In 1859, a man
named John Brown decided to fight slavery
by forming a group of armed men. John Brown
really hated the idea of slavery. He and his
band of men raided a place where the
government stored weapons in Harpers Ferry,
Virginia. John's plan was to steal weapons
and give them to slaves so they could fight
for their freedom.

U.S. Marines capture John Brown during his raid on Harpers Ferry.

What John Brown did was definitely against the law. President Buchanan sent the U.S. Marines in to capture him. John Brown ended up being captured, convicted, and hanged. People in the South thought John was a madman and got what he deserved. Many people in the North, however, thought John Brown was a brave hero.

Harriet Lane, James Buchanan's niece, served as First Lady during the Buchanan presidency.

It seemed that whatever President Buchanan did angered one group of people or another. The president became very cautious, and decided not to make many decisions at all. This ended up angering people even more. Soon it seemed as if no one was satisfied with the way President Buchanan was running things.

There were some bright spots during President Buchanan's four-year term, though.

One was his niece, Harriet Lane. Because he didn't have a wife, James asked Harriet to serve as the nation's First Lady. Harriet was very smart and pretty. She hosted terrific dinner parties at the White House. White House guests and newspaper reporters loved her. She often got more attention than her uncle.

The Coming and Going of the Pony Express, by Frederic Remington
(Gilcrease Museum, Tulsa, Oklahoma)

During the time when James Buchanan was president, there were also some big breakthroughs in communications. One was the Pony Express. With this new service, a brave group of young cowboys delivered mail across the West in just a few days instead of in weeks or months.

Another accomplishment of the time was the transatlantic telegraph cable. Much of the

cable stretched across the ocean floor. It was
a miraculous achievement that connected the
United States with England. People could now
communicate across the ocean with lightning
speed. Unfortunately, Buchanan didn't really
have much to do with these accomplishments
and couldn't take too much credit for them.

A photograph of James Buchanan during his later years

When President James Buchanan retired to his Pennsylvania home in 1861, seven southern states had already left the Union. In a few weeks, the Civil War would begin.

Many Americans blamed President Buchanan for not doing enough to stop the war. James Buchanan probably didn't do enough, but the United States was probably headed for civil war no matter who the president was. James Buchanan died in 1868 at the age of seventy-seven. He is remembered as one of Americas most unpopular presidents.